New Quilting

New Quilting

Isabel Stanley and Jenny Watson

SMITHMARK

THIS EDITION PUBLISHED IN 1997 BY SMITHMARK PUBLISHERS INC.
A DIVISION OF US MEDIA HOLDINGS INC.
16 EAST 32ND STREET, NEW YORK, NY 10016

SMITHMARK BOOKS ARE AVAILABLE FOR BULK PURCHASE FOR SALES PROMOTION
AND FOR PREMIUM USE. FOR DETAILS WRITE OR CALL THE MANAGER OF
SPECIAL SALES, SMITHMARK PUBLISHERS INC., 16 EAST 32ND STREET
NEW YORK, NY 10016: (212) 532-6600

ISBN 0-7651-9576-3

PUBLISHER: JOANNA LORENZ
PROJECT EDITOR: JUDITH SIMONS
PHOTOGRAPHER: GLORIA NICOL
STEP PHOTOGRAPHER: LUCY TIZARD
STYLIST: GLORIA NICOL
DESIGNER: LOUISE MORLEY
ILLUSTRATOR: LUCINDA GANDERTON

1 3 5 7 9 10 8 6 4 2

PRINTED AND BOUND IN HONG KONG

CONTENTS

· · · · · ·

INTRODUCTION
· · · · · ·

ABOVE: This delightful sea-inspired appliqué picture is full of contemporary style.

Textile crafts are constantly changing and evolving to fit the moods of fashion. After a decline in popularity, patchwork and appliqué were revived in the 1960s and '70s, together with interest in ethnic textiles and a fascination for the American pioneer lifestyle. During these two decades, patchwork garments were embroidered with motifs and sentimental or political slogans, in a similar fashion to the crazy patchwork quilts of the Victorian era.

The projects in this book update the textile traditions of the past. The colours and patterns are bold and dramatic, the motifs quirky and modern. Instructions are given for contemporary items such as rucksacks and T shirts, as well as modern interpretations of traditional items. For speed and convenience, block designs are used as single motifs and simplified for machine sewing. Mosaic patchwork, which is usually made up of hundreds of geometric shapes, has been re-designed and the patches enlarged to save time. Patches must be cut with exactly measured seam allowances for machine-sewn patchwork – accuracy is essential to ensure that all the shapes fit and the seams are aligned.

Using a sewing machine imposes certain constraints on patchwork design. Many-sided shapes are difficult to piece and joining curved seams is not easy. Smaller shapes are fiddly to work with and a diagonal patch will need careful stitching to prevent distortion. Iron-on interfacing, cut to the size of the finished patch and used as a backing, will not only stabilize the fabric but also serve as a guide for machine-stitching. The easiest shape to fit is a square or rectangle; these can be stitched into strips, and then the strips joined. For a beginner, the square is the ideal shape. Select two contrasting shades to create a bold checker board effect. Advanced needleworkers might like to design their own geometric patchwork, as it is, after all, a highly personal craft. Contemporary patchworkers have often been influenced by geometric

RIGHT: Hand-made paper is not the first appliqué material to spring to mind, but it can be utilized to produce beautiful contemporary items, such as this paper portfolio.

patterns found in other forms of decoration. Islamic architecture is particularly interesting for its colourful mosaics, stained glass and cut stone designs.

In these days of mass production, the desire to personalize textiles is strong, and there is a great deal of pleasure to be found in designing and making, and satisfaction in the completion of the work. Perhaps the most important consideration is that of time. We no longer wish to spend long hours on one item – most of us would prefer to start and finish a project in one day. Thankfully, developments in specialist materials and equipment help to minimize the time spent in preparation.

Iron-on fusible bonding web has revolutionized the art of appliqué. The immediacy of this method is extremely attractive, with the interfacing bonding one layer of fabric to another. Bonding agents, such as pastes and starches, have been used for many years, but the modern version is much simpler to use. Its main advantage is that it prevents fabric from puckering, fraying or shifting before or during stitching. As the interfacing is paper-backed, motifs can be easily traced on to it before application. It also lines the fabric, so a light fabric applied to a dark ground will not show through. Usually appliqué edges are neatened with a narrow machine satin stitch, but if the appliquéd item will only receive light wear then they may be hand-stitched. For really quick results, leave the edges of motifs unstitched and use pinking shears to prevent the edges from fraying.

Cotton fabrics are traditionally chosen for textile projects and are certainly the easiest to use. Select firmly woven fabric, and do not choose cottons with a high manmade content as they will not press well. Cotton fabrics are easy to wash, and are available in many colours and prints. More skilled needleworkers may be more adventurous. Contemporary textile artists use a variety of exciting fabrics such as PVC, plastics (acetates) and organza woven in silk and metallic fibres. For patchwork, you must use fabrics of equal weight, but for appliqué you can use almost any combination of weights. Other materials, such as paper and fur fabrics give texture, and you can recycle old woollen garments to make felt. Another short cut is to use felt as an appliqué fabric, as it non-woven and therefore does not fray. Felt is ideal for items that do not need laundering. Knitted or stretch fabrics are not suitable for appliqué or patchwork projects.

Seek out interesting trimmings, beads, sequins, buttons and ribbons to add detail to a piece. Specialist manufacturers also produce a variety of machine and hand embroidery threads, including neons and metallics. With the advances in synthetic dyes, there are an incredible range of shades.

ABOVE: A cot quilt with a folk motif, this is still a very up-to-date interpretation.

BELOW: Patchwork and appliqué techniques may be ages old, but the choice of fabrics and materials dictates this contemporary style.

TOOLS AND EQUIPMENT

Many needleworkers will already have most of the equipment listed here. However, the more specialist items are readily available from craft shops and department stores.

SCISSORS AND CUTTING TOOLS

Dressmaker's scissors or shears Use for cutting out fabric only, so as not to dull the blades.

Paper scissors Sharpen these regularly and only use for paper.

Embroidery scissors These small, sharp and sometimes decorative scissors are used in patchwork, quilting and appliqué to cut thread and trim fabric.

Pinking shears These scissors have serrated blades and are used to prevent fraying on cut edges and also for cutting decorative edges.

Rotary cutter This tool should always be used in conjunction with a cutting mat. Use to cut out patch pieces accurately. Check blades for any nicks and replace when necessary.

Craft knife Useful for cutting out cardboard or plastic (acetate) templates. Always cut away from the body.

MEASURING TOOLS

Metal-edged ruler Use when drafting templates and also when cutting cardboard and fabric with a rotary cutter or knife.

Metre rule Use together with a set square to cut lengths of fabric.

Set square Use to measure accurate right angles and use with a metre rule to cut lengths of fabric.

Tape measure A flexible measuring tool, useful for measuring lengths of fabric.

Pair of compasses Use for drawing circles.

MARKERS

Adjustable marker and gauge A useful tool for checking measurements.

Vanishing marker Marks made with this special marker will fade on contact with water or air and therefore can be used to mark designs on to fabric. A soft lead pencil can also be used, but only on the reverse of the fabric.

Dressmaker's wheel and chalk A piece of tailor's chalk can be used directly on fabric as it will brush off later. It can also be used in conjunction with a dressmaker's wheel for pouncing (see Basic Techniques).

SEWING EQUIPMENT

Needles "Sharps" are used for hand-sewing appliqué and patchwork and "betweens" for making smaller stitches.

Crewel needles These are used for working embroidery stitches and come in sizes 1 to 10. Use size 7 for cotton and sailcloth fabrics.

Pins Discard any blunt or rusty pins. Quilting pins are longer than dressmaker's pins and pass through several layers of fabric easily.

Safety pins These are sometimes used in place of pins to hold together several layers of a quilt.

Beeswax Run the wax along quilting thread before stitching so that the thread passes smoothly though the fabric.

Thimble These are essential, especially for hand quilting where the needle has to be pushed through several layers at once.

Unpicker An essential tool used to rip out machine stitches.

Iron Essential for pressing patchwork seams. If possible, use a steam iron to press seams and remove wrinkles. Otherwise use a dry iron with a damp pressing cloth.

HOOPS AND FRAMES

Embroidery hoop Two tightly fitting rings hold the fabric taut. Plastic hoops with a metal spring closure are recommended for use under the sewing machine. Use a large wooden hoop.

Embroidery frame These four-sided frames can be either freestanding or hand-held. Fabric is tightened by adjusting the side rollers.

MISCELLANEOUS

Fabric glue This may be used in place of fusible bonding web to secure appliqué to the ground fabric.

Paper glue Spray glue is recommended for making templates.

Fabric paints and dyes Painted fabrics may be quilted and water-based non-toxic paints which are fixed by ironing are recommended. Use fabric dyes to create unusual colours, or to unify fabrics. Both hot and cold water dyes are available, although cold dyes need to be fixed. Follow the manufacturer's instructions.

KEY:
1   Dressmaker's scissors or shears
2   Embroidery scissors
3   Pinking shears
4   Rotary cutter
5   Craft knife
6   Metal-edged ruler
7   Metre rule
8   Tape measure
9   Set square
10 Pair of compasses
11 Adjustable marker and gauge
12 Vanishing marker
13 Dressmaker's chalk
14 Needles
15 Beeswax
16 Quilting pins
17 Safety pins
18 Thimble
19 Unpicker
20 Embroidery hoop
21 Large hoop for quilting
22 Fabric glue
23 Fabric paints and dyes

MATERIALS
· · · · · ·

Most of the following materials are standard items used regularly in needlework. More specialist items are available from craft shops or department stores.

Acid-free paper Use to wrap textiles for safe storage.

Beads and sequins Choose from a wide selection of materials, including glass, wood, plastic and bone.

Bias binding This is a narrow strip of fabric used to cover raw edges. It can be purchased ready-made or hand-made (see Basic Techniques).

Buttons Choose from a wide variety of materials, including plastic, mother-of-pearl, wood or fabric-covered. Used as fastenings for clothing, buttons can also be used for decoration or to fasten quilts and cushions.

Dressmaker's carbon paper This is used to transfer designs to fabric.

Embroidery threads Choose from pearl cotton, a high sheen 2-ply thread; stranded embroidery thread, a 5-ply thread (separate the strands for fine work); machine embroidery thread, available in various weights and a full range of colours including metallic.

Eyelets (grommets) Available in kit form, these are used to thread cord or ribbon through for a tie fastening.

Iron-on fusible bonding web This bonds two layers of fabric together and is often used to bond an appliqué motif to the ground fabric. Templates can be traced on to the backing paper.

Iron-on interfacing Lightweight interfacing can be used on the wrong side of patch pieces to mark out the seam line for machine stitching. It can also be used to back fabric.

Isometric, graph or squared dressmaker's paper Use to accurately draw a motif or template.

Lace Strips of lace or patches of lace can be used to embellish appliqué.

Press studs (snap fasteners) These metallic fasteners can be used to secure two pieces of fabric together, such as a cushion cover opening.

Ribbon This can be used to embellish appliqué or crazy patchwork or to edge a border. Choose from a variety of materials, including velvet, satin or man-made fabric.

Stuffing This is used to fill cushions and soft toys and is made from cotton, wool and synthetic fibres.

Thread For hand-sewing, use 100% cotton thread, and for machine-sewing use 100% cotton or a polyester blend. Tacking (basting) thread is stronger than sewing thread and is used for temporarily securing layers of fabric. Quilting thread is also much stronger.

Tissue paper This is used for transferring designs and also for holding appliqué shapes together.

Tracing paper Use to trace off a design.

Trimmings These are used to make unusual edgings or to embellish a quilt or patchwork piece. Examples include fringing, pompon tape, tassels and flat ribbon tape.

Wadding (batting) This soft fabric is used as a middle layer for quilts and for filling trapunto designs. It is usually made from cotton, but is also available in silk, wool and synthetics.

Yarn Used in quilting to fill a corded quilt. It is also used for embroidery stitches and knitting.

Zip (zipper) Used to close together two open edges.

KEY:
1 Acid-free paper
2 Wadding (batting)
3 Beads and sequins
4 Bias binding
5 Buttons
6 Dressmaker's carbon paper
7 Eyelets (grommets)
8 Embroidery threads
9 Machine embroidery thread
10 Graph paper
11 Iron-on fusible bonding web
12 Iron-on interfacing
13 Lace
14 Stuffing
15 Press studs (snap fasteners)
16 Ribbon
17 Stencil card
18 Sewing thread
19 Tacking (basting) thread
20 Trimmings
21 Yarn

FABRICS

Many different types of fabric can be employed in patchwork, quilting and appliqué work. Detailed information on choosing fabric designs for your work is given in the following pages.

Calico A strong, plain-weave fabric, usually white or natural with darker flecks; available in a variety of weights.

Corduroy/needlecord (fine-wale corduroy) A plain-weave fabric with vertical pile-effect ribbing. Although it frays easily, it is suitable for appliqué and large-scale patch pieces.

Cotton Woven from the raw material, cotton is hard-wearing, and launders and presses well. Available in a wide range of plain and patterned print colours, this is the best choice for patchwork.

Felt This non-woven fabric is made from wool by compressing the fibres with moisture and heat. Felt shrinks, so is not suitable for articles that need regular washing. However, it is ideal for appliqué work as it does not fray.

Gingham Alternating stripes of coloured and white threads in the warp and weft produce this checked pattern in cotton or cotton blend fabric.

Lawn A fine crisp cotton, or cotton blend fabric, this is available in printed designs and plain colours.

Linen Woven from a natural fibre produced by the flax plant, the variable thickness of the yarn produces an uneven and attractive appearance to the fabric. Linen frays and creases easily, but is suitable as a ground fabric.

Muslin A white or natural open-weave cotton or cotton blend fabric, this is suitable for backing trapunto or corded quilts, shadow quilting and appliqué.

Organdy This fine cotton fabric is starched and is suitable for shadow work.

Organza A gauzy, crisp fabric woven from silk or synthetic fibres or a silk and synthetic blend. Available in plain colours, and with metallic and iridescent effects, it is suitable for appliqué and shadow work. It can also be used for delicate patchwork.

PVC/poly vinyl chloride (acetate) This plastic, cotton-backed cloth is not flexible like ordinary fabrics so is difficult to work with. However, it can be used for patchwork and appliqué if you lubricate your sewing machine and the machine foot before stitching.

Sateen This soft fabric has surface sheen and is more subtle than cotton or cotton blend fabrics. It is used in patchwork and is a popular choice for quilting.

Satin This shiny fabric can be woven from cotton, silk or synthetics. It frays and creases easily, but can be used to good effect in patchwork and appliqué.

Silk The queen of fabrics, silk works well for almost any project. Woven from the natural fibre produced by the silk worm, silk fabrics are lustrous and available in a wide variety of textures, colours, patterns and weights.

Shantung Woven with yarns of irregular thickness, giving an uneven surface, shantung fabric frays easily but can be used for patchwork and quilting.

Taffeta This is a plain-weave fabric with a two-tone effect. Produced in both natural and synthetic silk fibres, it is suitable for appliqué and especially effective in small patchwork.

Velvet Produced in cotton, cotton blend and synthetics, this fabric has a closely woven backing and a dense cut-pile surface. Dress velvet is lighter and more lustrous but frays easily and is difficult to handle. The fabric nap must always lie in the same direction for patchwork.

Voile This fine woven fabric is translucent and often used for shadow work. Cotton voile is finer and easier to work with than synthetic varieties.

Wool Made from woven fleece, the natural fibre has a springy texture and insulating properties. Synthetic blends mimic these properties well. However, wool does not launder easily because it is prone to shrinkage. Suitable for inlaid appliqué, light weights can also be used for patchwork.

KEY:

1 Corduroy/ needlecord (fine-wale corduroy)	7 Organza
	8 PVC/poly vinyl chloride (acetate)
2 Cotton	9 Satin
3 Felt	10 Silk
4 Gingham	11 Taffeta
5 Linen	12 Velvet
6 Organdy	13 Wool

BASIC TECHNIQUES

· · · · · ·

The many varied projects in this book feature a wealth of design ideas employing a wide range of techniques, both old and modern, and from all four corners of the world. You will discover the secrets of appliqué work with PVC and strip patchwork, along with filling patterns, mosaic effects and much more. However, there are many standard quilting, patchwork and appliqué techniques that need to be grasped before you begin a project – you will be coming across the same methods again and again, both in this book and in any original creative work that you are inspired to try.

PATCHWORK TECHNIQUES

Pieced patchwork is made from fabric scraps which are cut into regular shapes and then sewn together in geometric patterns to form a mosaic of cloth. The patches can be pieced or joined together by one of two basic methods: by machine or by hand. Machining is quickest, but hand sewing gives a traditional look to a finished piece with slightly irregular seams. For the beginner, working over backing papers is the best way to make precise angled shapes when piecing by hand. Whichever method is chosen, accurate templates, meticulous measuring and cutting, careful stitching and thorough pressing are all vital for a professional finish.

TEMPLATES

Accurate templates will allow you to make patches identical in size and shape that will fit perfectly together. There are several different types of template you can make or buy. You can cut them yourself from card (cardboard) or from firm, clear plastic (acetate). Alternatively, you can make window templates, which allow you to view the fabric. Always make a new template for each shape required in a project – old templates eventually become a little distorted round the edges. Templates can also be purchased ready-made in various shapes and sizes.

Patchwork templates should always include a seam allowance; in this book the seam allowance is usually 5 mm (¼ in). If you are using backing papers, you will need to cut two templates if using card or plastic – one with the seam allowance included for marking the fabric and one without the seam allowance for the backing paper. If using a window template, the outside edge of the frame is used to mark the fabric and the inside edge of the frame the backing paper.

MAKING CARD (CARDBOARD) TEMPLATES

1

Transfer the design on to squared paper and cut round each shape with a sharp pair of scissors.

2

Glue the shapes to a piece of thin card (cardboard), and draw a seam allowance round each. Cut out the card.

3

Protect the seam allowance area with a thin coat of clear nail varnish.

MAKING PLASTIC (ACETATE) TEMPLATES

Place the clear plastic (acetate) over the design and draw round each shape. Then draw a seam allowance round each and cut out. Being transparent, the template can be accurately positioned on the fabric.

MAKING WINDOW TEMPLATES

Trace the shape on to card (cardboard), then draw a 5 mm (¼ in) seam allowance round it. Cut out the outer and inner parts, leaving a card frame the exact width of the seam allowance.

MAKING CURVED TEMPLATES

For curved blocks, mark notches on the seam lines of the pattern before cutting it into sections. Cut out each template and then carefully cut out the notches with a craft knife.

PREPARING PATCHES

Position the template on the fabric, lining up one straight edge with the grain of the fabric. Draw round it on to the reverse of the fabric using a vanishing marker, tailor's chalk or a soft pencil. Butt the shapes together to ensure a good fit.

CUTTING OUT PATCHES IN GROUPS

1

Several patches can be cut at once using this method. Fold the fabric like a concertina and then staple the card (cardboard) template to the layers.

2

Use a sharp rotary cutter or a craft knife and press hard into the cutting mat.

3

Organize the cut pieces by stringing them on a length of thread. You can store them like this and remove them one at a time.

ATTACHING BACKING PAPERS

Pin the backing papers to the reverse of the fabric patches. Fold over or press the seam allowance. Leaving a short free end of thread, tack (baste) along the middle of the seam allowance to the end of the side and trim the corners. Fold over the adjacent seam allowance and continue to tack. Repeat on all sides, leaving the thread ends free so that the threads and the backing papers can be removed easily once the work has been pieced.

BACKING WITH INTERFACING

Iron-on interfacing can be used instead of backing papers. It is especially useful when machine piecing. Mark the patches on the interfacing adjacent to one another. Cut along the main lines first and then cut out the individual blocks. Iron these on to the reverse of the fabric, then mark a seam allowance round the interfacing on the fabric. Cut out the patches individually with scissors or as a group with a rotary cutter.

PIECING OR JOINING PATCHES

Lay out the cut patches to work out the final arrangement. When you are happy with the design, you can begin piecing the patches. There are several different methods of doing this, depending on whether you are piecing by hand or using a sewing machine.

HAND PIECING

Right sides facing, pin the prepared patches together. First pin each corner, and then pin at equidistant points along the side. Join the patches with a small, neat whip stitch – or overstitch – as shown. Insert the needle in one corner and work across to the other, removing the pins as you go.

MACHINE PIECING PATCHES BY THE FLAG METHOD

The flag method enables you to join several pairs of patches in one go. Right sides facing, pin the patches in pairs. Stitch along the seam line using the presser foot as a guide, removing the pins as you go. Leave a short uncut thread between each pair. Remove the flags and cut into units. Join enough pairs to make up the patched piece. To avoid bulk, always press the patch seams flat to one side and not open as in dressmaking.

JOINING PATCHES INTO ROWS

For both hand and machine piecing, make sure that the seam allowances match up perfectly before you pin and stitch the rows together. Press the seams in opposite directions to reduce bulk.

SETTING-IN — BOX PATCHWORK

Setting-in is the term used when a patch is sewn into an angle. To make the angled piece, stitch two pieces together along the seam line, stop stitching 5mm (¼ in) from the end of the seam, and secure with back stitch. Right sides facing, pin one angled piece to the edge of the patch. Stitch from the corner out to the edge, then swing the adjacent angled piece to the other side of the patch, again stitching from the corner out. Press the two seam allowances of the set-in patch toward the angled piece.

SASHING AND BORDERS

These are two very different things although they are cut and sewn in the same way. Sashings are fabric strips used within a design to separate individual patches, or blocks of patches. Borders go round the edges of the work to cover and hide any raw edges.

BLOCKED BORDERS

For the long sides of a border, cut the strips the same length as the quilt. For the short sides, cut the strips the width of the quilt plus the double width of the border. Right sides facing, sew the long strips to the piece first, and then the short strips. Press the seam allowance away from the direction of quilting.

BORDERS WITH MITRED CORNERS

Cut the border strips as above, adding an extra 5 cm (2 in) to all four for mitring, and stitch to the quilt in the usual way. To mitre a corner by hand, press a border strip down at a 45 degree angle, pin and slip stitch on the right side to secure in place. To mitre by machine, work from the wrong side, pressing all the corners back at a 45 degree angle. Pin together and stitch along the fold. Trim the seam allowance and press flat.

LOG CABIN PATCHWORK

Always work from the middle out. Starting with a central square, pin and stitch strips to the square one by one, trimming each strip to the centre as you go. Work round the block anti-clockwise – each new strip will be slightly longer than the previous one. Continue adding strips until you reach the required size. Edge with mitred borders. Often several Log Cabin blocks are made and then stitched together to make a quilt.

QUILTING TECHNIQUES

Quilts are made from three layers: a top piece which is decorated, a layer of wadding (batting) for warmth and a backing piece. These layers are held together with lines of stitching which can be worked in a grid, straight rows or elaborate patterns. Quilted borders, medallions, knots and detailed corners are all possible. Originally, lines of tiny running stitches were worked to offer more warmth. Modern technology and new fibres have made this unnecessary, although the stitches still need to be of equal length.

TACKING (BASTING) QUILTS

Sandwich the wadding (batting) between the top piece and the backing, with the fabrics right side out. Tack (baste) together securely. Knot a long length of thread in a contrasting colour. Work from the middle out, tacking the layers together horizontally, vertically and diagonally. If quilting by machine or with a hoop, add extra lines round the edges.

HAND QUILTING

Place the inner hoop on a flat surface, lay the tacked fabric on top. Place the outer hoop over both and screw the nut to tighten the hoop. Stitch from the top, using your free hand to guide the needle up and down through the layers below.

MACHINE QUILTING

For quilting grids and straight lines, a quilting foot will allow the machine to move more easily over thick fabrics. For free-form quilting, remove the foot and lower the foot lever. Stretch the fabric taut either with a hoop or your hands, and stitch slowly so that you can accurately guide the stitches.

APPLIQUÉ TECHNIQUES

Appliqué can be worked in a variety of fabrics, including silk, wool and cotton, and strong, closely woven fabric is possibly the best choice. Felt is popular for appliqué designs because it does not fray. Design ideas are limitless and virtually any shape can be used.

IRON-ON FUSIBLE BONDING WEB

1

A quick and easy way to attach appliqué to the fabric. Because the appliqué fabric is fused to the web, it won't fray. Trace the outline on to the fusible web.

2

Roughly cut out the design and iron this on to the fabric. Cut round the outline with a sharp pair of scissors, a rotary cutter or craft knife.

3

Peel off the backing paper and iron, fusing the motif to the main fabric. Set the machine to a zig zag and stitch round the raw edge of the motif.

PIN TACKING (BASTING)

BELOW: This simple appliqué sunflower has been stitched on by hand.

Tack (baste) the seam allowance round the appliqué design. Mark the placement lines on the right side of the fabric. Arrange the appliqué shapes on the fabric following these lines. First position the background pieces, and then layer any extra pieces on top. Alternatively, attach the pieces with double-sided tape.

STITCHES

Straight stitch is the standard machine sewing stitch, worked in straight lines and secured by back stitch at the end of each seam. Machine tacking stitches are worked by setting the machine to the longest stitch. To attach appliqué and crazy patchwork, set the machine to a close zig zag stitch and work a row of satin stitches. The following hand stitches are used throughout the book.

RUNNING STITCH

This is the main stitch used for hand quilting. It is also used for sewing seams in patchwork and quilting. Stitches should be of an even length, no bigger than 3 mm (⅛ in), and can be run a few at a time. Running stitch is also used in sashiko and kantha work.

HOLBEIN STITCH

Work a row of running stitch in one direction and then fill in the spaces on the return journey.

SLIP-STITCH

This stitch is used to secure a finished edge to another surface, like an appliqué or a binding. With the needle, catch a thread under the fabric together with a single thread on the fold of the fabric, spacing these small stitches evenly apart.

WHIP STITCH

Also known as oversewing and overcasting, this small straight stitch is used to hold together two edges. Work from back to front, inserting the needle at an angle and picking up a thread from each piece at the same time.

STAB STITCH

This stitch replaces running stitch when quilting thick fabric. Hold the needle perpendicular to the fabric, and work one stitch at a time. It is also used to outline individual shapes on quilted fabric.

BLANKET STITCH

Blanket, or buttonhole, stitch is ideal for finishing off raw or scalloped edges on fabrics that don't fray, such as felt or blanket. It can also be worked over a fold. Insert the needle into the back so that it points up to the raw edge, wind the loose thread over the needle and pull through the loop. Make a decorative feature of large blanket stitches by sewing them in a contrasting colour.

GENERAL TECHNIQUES

· · · · · ·

FINDING THE GRAIN OF THE FABRIC

It is necessary to find the grain to straighten raw edges. Nick the fabric just below the raw edge, pull a thread gently across the fabric and cut along the line made. You can pull threads to fringe a piece of fabric and also to mark a grid. Sometimes you will need to find the straight grain in order to centre a motif.

ENLARGING A DESIGN

Trace the motif on to squared paper. On another sheet of paper, mark out the same number of squares to the required size of the finished design. Copy the motif on to the new grid so that the lines of the design correspond exactly with the original.

TRANSFERRING A DESIGN
ON TO FABRIC

<u>1</u>

Copy the design on to dressmaker's carbon paper. Place the carbon on the reverse of the fabric and then trace over the outline with a pen, pressing heavily.

<u>2</u>

Pouncing is used to transfer a design on to the right side of the fabric for an appliqué or quilting design. Trace over the design on to paper with a dressmaker's wheel or an unthreaded sewing machine, so that the design appears as a broken line. Push tailor's chalk through the pierced paper with a brush or sponge to mark the fabric.

<u>3</u>

Trace the design on to tissue paper, pin to the wrong side of the fabric then machine round the outline. Rip away the tissue paper to reveal the outline. This method is good for fine or fragile fabric.

BELOW: This drawstring bag shows designs transferred on to the patchwork squares.

MAKING AND USING BIAS STRIPS

Bias strips are used for binding, piping and also in the stained glass appliqué method. Cut a square on the straight grain, fold it in half diagonally and stitch together the open edges. Press the seam allowance flat and trim. Mark parallel lines on to the fabric and then roll it into a tube so that the top edge aligns with the first marked line. Pin and stitch along this line. Press the seam flat and trim. Cut along the marked lines into one long continuous strip of bias binding. Alternatively, cut several strips on the diagonal and then join them together, pressing the seam allowance flat.

BINDING A MITRED CORNER

<u>1</u>

Stitch along one edge, reducing the size of the stitches near the corner. Stop stitching 5 mm (¼ in) from the corner, lift the presser foot and swivel the quilt to stitch the next edge. A tuck will form in the binding at the corner. Lower the presser foot, and carry on stitching the next side.

<u>2</u>

Fold over the binding, pin and sew close to the previous stitching line. Fold the tuck diagonally to mitre the corners and slip-stitch in place.

ENVELOPE CUSHION COVER

For the front, cut a square to fit the cushion pad, adding 1 cm (½ in) seam allowance on all sides. Cut a back piece 2.5 cm (1 in) bigger on one side, and then cut in half lengthways. Press, and sew a 1 cm (½ in) hem along the cut edge of both back pieces. Right sides facing, pin the front to the back pieces so that one hem lies slightly over the other. Sew round all four seams and, if directed, stitch in piping or fringing now. Clip the corners, press and turn right side out.

STRETCHING AND MOUNTING A PICTURE

Stretch the finished piece taut over the backing. Using a strong thread, stitch back and forth, joining the raw edges in a criss cross pattern and pulling the thread tightly as you go. Work the long sides first, then repeat with the short sides. Secure to the backing board with tape.

DRAWSTRING BAG

<u>1</u>

Pin together two rectangles in main fabric and sew round three sides, leaving the top short side open. Cut two rectangles the same size in lining and stitch the two long sides. Stitch part way across the short end, break off for 5 cm (2 in), then stitch to the end. Right sides facing, pin the two bags together and stitch a continuous line round the top edge. Trim and clip the seam. Pull the bag through the lining. Press and slip-stitch to close the gap.

<u>2</u>

Push the lining into the bag and press flat. For the channel, machine stitch two parallel lines, 1 cm (½ in) from the top edge and 1 cm (½ in) apart. Make a hole in the seam between the two rows of stitching with a stitch unpicker and thread the drawstring through.

PEG BAG

· · · · · ·

This peg bag is made from patchwork triangles placed in alternating colours to look like a windmill.
Choose a contrasting piece of printed fabric to make up the bag.

PREPARATION

YOU WILL NEED

· · · · · ·

*40 cm x 90 cm (16 in x
36 in) printed cotton fabric*

dressmaker's scissors

paper and pencil

card (cardboard)

craft knife

*1 m x 90 cm (1 yd x 36 in)
green cotton fabric*

*50 cm x 90 cm (20 in x
36 in) yellow cotton fabric*

dressmaker's pins

*sewing machine and
zipper foot*

matching thread

*1 m x 90 cm
(1 yd x 36 in) piping cord*

*37 cm (15 in) wooden
coat hanger*

Enlarge the diagram from the back of the book on to paper and cut out two sides, one top and one back in printed fabric, adding a 1 cm (½ in) seam allowance. Enlarge the triangle motif and make a card (cardboard) template. Cut four triangles in green, and four in yellow, adding a 5mm (¼ in) seam allowance. To make the piping, cut a 8 cm x 65 cm (3 in x 26 in) bias strip from yellow fabric (see Basic Techniques). Join it into a circle and press the seam open.

1

Join the triangles, alternating the colours as shown, to form a square patch. Clip and press the seams to one side.

2

Right sides facing, machine the patch to the side pieces. Press the seams open. Attach the top piece the same way, trim and press the seams flat towards the top.

3

Fold the piping strip lengthways. Attach the zipper foot and stitch, enclosing the piping cord. Tack (baste) the piping strip to the opening, with the sewing line matching the seam. Stitch and clip the curved edge. Press under the piping seam allowance, trim and slip-stitch.

4

Right sides facing, match the front to the back, then stitch round the edge of the bag.

TO FINISH

Clip the corners, turn right side out and press flat. Push the hanger wire through the centre top seam.

CHILD'S BERET

· · · · · ·

This PVC beret with a colourful daisy appliqué will brighten up a rainy day. Alternatively, buy a ready-made beret and sew the daisy motif on to it.

YOU WILL NEED

· · · · · ·

paper and pencil

paper scissors

tracing paper

dressmaker's scissors

10 cm x 90 cm (4 in x 36 in) iron-on interfacing

iron

assorted scraps of fabric

50 cm x 90 cm (20 in x 36 in) red PVC

50 cm x 90 cm (20 in x 36 in) polka dot cotton fabric

dressmaker's pins

embroidery thread

crewel needle

sewing machine and matching thread

PREPARATION

Enlarge the templates and cut out in paper. Draw the daisy shapes on to tracing paper and transfer to the interfacing. Cut out the shapes, iron to the fabric scraps and cut out. Cut a circle in red PVC measuring 40 cm (16 in), and one in polka dot cotton for the lining. Cut a hat band, 5 cm (2 in) wide and 4 cm (1¾ in) larger than the head measurement, in both fabrics.

1

Position the daisy in the centre of the red PVC circle. Pin and blanket stitch in place, then add diagonal stitches on either side.

2

Join the short ends of the hat bands, trim and clip. Place the red PVC and the lining together, wrong sides facing, and pleat at the back of the beret. Pin the pleats, and adjust to the size of the bands.

3

Stitch the PVC band to the pleated circle, then sew the second band to the first. Trim the seams and press flat. Fold the band to the wrong side and stitch.

25%

SCOTTIE DOG T SHIRT

Decorate a plain T shirt with this Scottie dog motif. Alternatively, appliqué the motif on to a pair of dungarees (overalls).

YOU WILL NEED
• • • • • •

iron

iron-on fusible bonding web

fabric scrap

paper and pencil

dressmaker's scissors

child's T shirt

needle and matching thread

13 cm (5 in) tartan ribbon

glass bead

embroidery thread

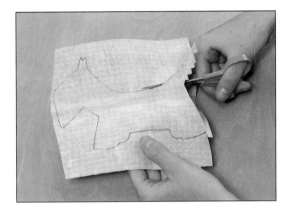

1

Iron the bonding web to the reverse of the fabric scrap. Enlarge the template and draw it on to the bonding web. Cut out the dog.

2

Peel off the backing, position the dog and iron in place. Slip-stitch to the T shirt.

3

Tie the ribbon into a bow and stitch to the dog's neck. Stitch on the bead for the eye, and work a few stitches for the mouth.

50%

BLACK-AND-WHITE APPLIQUÉ COVER

This striking design plays on positive and negative images. The design is cut out in black and white, and then appliquéd on to the reverse squares.

YOU WILL NEED
• • • • • •

3 cm (12½ in) square card (cardboard) and pencil

craft knife

1.5 m x 115 cm (1½ yd x 45 in) calico fabric

dressmaker's scissors

2 m x 115 cm (2¼ yd x 45 in) black cotton fabric

102 cm x 90 cm (40 in x 36 in) iron-on fusible bonding web

iron

sewing machine and black thread

PREPARATION

Enlarge the template on to the card and cut round the outline. Cut 12 calico and six black cotton 32 cm (12½ in) squares. Cut the bonding web into six 32 cm (12½ in) squares. Cut a backing piece in black cotton 98 cm x 1.3 m (39 in x 52 in).

1

Draw round the template on to each of the bonding web squares.

2

Iron the bonding web to the reverse of the black squares and carefully cut out the design.

3

Peel off the backing papers and arrange the pieces from each black square on to two calico squares. Use the template as a guide for positioning the individual black pieces. Iron on.

25%

TO FINISH

Using the flag method (see Basic Techniques), stitch the 12 squares into blocks of three. Stitch the blocks into four rows. Wrong sides facing, tack the cover to the backing piece. Bring the backing over to the front, mitre the corners (see Basic Techniques) and top stitch to the cover.

4

Set the machine to zig zag and stitch round the black shapes.

SILK CHRISTMAS CARDS

· · · · · ·

These Christmas trees are made from strips of checked silk sewn together and cut into triangles. This simple patchwork technique is very effective.

YOU WILL NEED

· · · · · ·

pencil and ruler

assorted scraps of checked silk fabric

dressmaker's scissors

sewing machine and contrasting thread

dressmaker's pins

fabric glue

card (cardboard)

paper scissors

1

Cut the silk into strips 2.5 cm x 36 cm (1 in x 14 in). Over-lap the strips and then stitch together lengthways using a contrasting thread.

2

Cut the patchwork piece into triangular shapes. Using a pin, draw threads from the raw edges to fringe each layer.

3

Glue each triangle to a piece of silk backing fabric, then glue to a piece of card and cut out. Cut pieces of card (card-board) and fold in half to make cards. Glue the trees on to the front of each card.

JAM JAR COVER

Appliqué this juicy strawberry on to a jam jar cover and embellish it with a few embroidery stitches. Make more covers and appliqué with a variety of fruits.

PREPARATION

Draw round a saucer on to both the pink and green fabrics and cut out two circles. Iron the bonding web on to scraps of fabric. Trace the strawberry motif on to paper, transfer on to the bonding web and cut out. Peel off the backing, centre the motif on the green fabric and iron on.

<u>1</u>

Outline the strawberry with colourful stitches. Embellish with cross stitches. Right sides facing, machine stitch the circles together, leaving a small gap.

<u>2</u>

Turn right side out. Sew running stitch round the edge. Attach the ribbon 5 cm (2 in) from the edge, place on a jam jar and tie in a bow.

29

APPLIQUÉ GLASSES CASE
· · · · · ·

By throwing old woollen knitwear into the washing machine, you can create a fabric with the flexibility of wool and the texture of felt. Draw motifs of your choice freehand and appliqué on to a glasses case.

YOU WILL NEED
· · · · ·

paper and pencil

paper scissors

assorted scraps of felted knitting

dressmaker's scissors

20 cm x 90 cm (8 in x 36 in) silk lining fabric

dressmaker's pins

sewing machine and matching thread

20 cm (8 in) braid

50 cm (½ yd) cord

PREPARATION

Enlarge the case template on to paper. Cut out a felted cover and a lining, plus four different-coloured felt squares to fit the cover.

1
Pin and sew the four felt squares on to the felted cover.

2
Cut out your selected motifs in felted scraps. Arrange them on the squares and pin.

3
Machine zig zag round the edges of the motifs.

4
Right sides facing, fold the case in half lengthways and stitch the seam. Turn right side out. Bind the top edge with the braid. Stitch the cord to the top.

25%

JEWELLERY ROLL
. . . . . .

This jewellery roll has been machine quilted in a meandering filling stitch. Filling patterns can be used to cover the whole area or to fill in a background. They can be as simple or as complex as you wish.

YOU WILL NEED
. . . . . .

20 cm x 90 cm (8 in x 36 in) checked silk fabric

dressmaker's scissors

scrap of wadding (batting)

needle and tacking (basting) thread

sewing machine and thread

1m (1 yd) bias binding

2 press studs (snap fasteners)

dressmaker's pins

zipper foot

15 cm (6 in) zip (zipper)

button

PREPARATION

Cut two pieces of silk and one piece of wadding (batting) 18 cm x 40 cm (7 in x 16 in). Sandwich the wadding between the two pieces of silk, with the silk right side out. Tack (baste) together, starting in the middle. Cut two 23 cm (9 in) lengths of bias binding and stitch together to make one wide strip. Cut in half, turn under the ends and stitch. Sew a press stud (snap fastener) to each end.

TO FINISH

Roll up the case and mark the centre of the long edge. Sew on a button and button loop.

1

Attach the darning foot to the machine and fill the whole quilted silk piece with a meandering filling stitch – a continuous wavy line. Use a contrasting coloured thread, or pick out one of the colours in the fabric.

2

Attach ordinary bias binding to the short ends. Fold the edges over by 7.5 cm (3 in) and tack (baste). Pin the zip (zipper) to one bound edge and stitch. Stitch the other side of the zip to the case. Divide the other pocket into three with vertical stitch lines.

3

Pin the wide strip of bias binding across the middle of the case. Pin strips of bias binding to the long ends of the case, and stitch. Trim the edges, fold the binding to the right side, and top stitch.

1950s' Bistro Placemat

This placemat has been appliquéd with a retro design of garden vegetables. This kitsch style is typical of kitchen design in the 1950s.

You Will Need

paper and pencil

paper scissors

dressmaker's pins

red, orange and yellow fabric scraps

dressmaker's scissors

20 cm x 50 cm (8 in x 20 in) green-and-red striped fabric

10 cm x 27 cm (4 in x 10½ in) yellow gingham fabric

needle and tacking (basting) thread

vanishing marker

green and brown embroidery thread

crewel needle

sewing machine and matching thread

iron

5 cm x 36 cm (2 in x 14 in) red cotton fabric

30 cm x 36 cm (12 in x 14 in) green gingham fabric

33 cm x 42 cm (13 in x 16½ in) single-sided quilted backing fabric

Preparation

Enlarge the motifs from the back of the book and cut out paper templates. Pin to the scraps and cut out, adding a 5 mm (¼ in) seam allowance. Cut two green-and-red striped fabric strips 5.5 cm x 9 cm (2¼ in x 3½ in), and one 7 cm x 36 cm (2¾ in x 14 in).

1

Clip and turn under the seam allowances on the fabric motifs and tack (baste). Cut three 10 cm x 9 cm (4 in x 3½ in) rectangles from the yellow gingham fabric.

2

Tack one vegetable to each rectangle and slip-stitch in place. Mark details with a vanishing marker. Hand stitch with embroidery thread.

3

Right sides facing, stitch the two short striped strips between the appliquéd patches and press flat. Then stitch the red strip to the left edge and the long green-and-red striped strip to the right edge.

4

Right sides facing, stitch the green gingham to the red strip. Stitch one short end of the quilted fabric to the long striped strip. Tack the top to the backing. Trim the mat to 32 cm x 42 cm (13 in x 16½ in). Cut the remaining striped fabric into strips and bind the other three edges.

APPLIQUÉ BOOK COVER

Personalize a notebook with this fabric cover. Felt is a good choice for appliqué as it does not fray.
Embellish the flower centre with coloured beads.

YOU WILL NEED
· · · · · ·

paper and pencil

paper scissors

*cotton fabric in two
contrasting colours*

dressmaker's scissors

assorted felt scraps

fabric glue

dressmaker's pins

*sewing machine and
matching thread*

iron

embroidery thread

crewel needle

coloured beads

PREPARATION

Lay the open book flat on paper and draw round it, adding a 1 cm (½ in) seam allowance. Pin the template to one fabric and cut out. Fold the template in half and cut out two pieces in contrasting fabric, adding an extra 1 cm (½ in) seam allowance to the folded edge. Enlarge the flower motif, draw on to a scrap of felt and cut out. Centre on the right hand side of the first piece of fabric and glue. Cut a flower centre in a different colour felt and glue to the flower.

50%

1

Turn under a hem on the long edges of the two contrasting fabric pieces. Stitch and press. Right sides facing, pin to the main piece.

2

Starting at the centre, machine stitch the seams. Clip the corners, press and turn right side out. Position the flower motif on the book cover and stitch round the edge. Stitch the beads to the flower centre.

VALENTINE CARD AND GIFT TAG
· · · · · · ·

Make a Valentine card and matching gift tag for a special friend and appliqué them with decorative heart motifs.

YOU WILL NEED
· · · · · ·

coloured card (cardboard)

pencil and ruler

paper scissors

hole punch

assorted fabric scraps

dressmaker's scissors

paper

fabric glue

dressmaker's pins

embroidery thread

crewel needle

small coloured beads

10 cm (4 in) gift cord

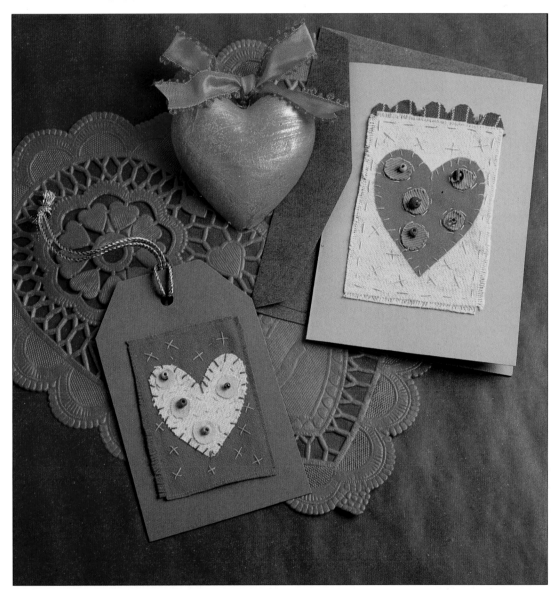

PREPARATION

Cut a piece of card (cardboard) 15 cm x 20 cm (6 in x 8 in) and fold in half. Cut another piece the same shape as a luggage label and punch a hole in the top. Cut two rectangles from the fabric to suit the size of your card and gift tag. Fray the edges of the fabric using a needle. Cut a strip of fabric with a scalloped edge and glue to the larger rectangular scrap. Enlarge and make a paper template of the heart motif.

50%

1

Pin the heart motifs to contrasting scraps of fabric, and cut out. Cut several small circles in contrasting colours.

2

Glue the circles to the hearts then glue the hearts on to the rectangles. Embellish with beads and colourful stitches. Glue the finished rectangles on to the card and the gift tag. Thread the gift tag with cord and knot.

APPLIQUÉ FELT HAT
· · · · · ·

This hat is made from felted scraps of knitting. Cool colours which recede, like blues and greens, will look good for the base. In contrast, use hot colours like pink, orange and red for the motifs.

PREPARATION

Enlarge the paper templates for the hat crown and band and cut out in paper. Cut the pieces out in both felted fabric and lining. Cut out enough felt squares in different colours to fit the band. Draw a design for the crown freehand and cut out in assorted colours of felt.

1

Pin the squares on to the band and zig zag stitch in place. Position your design on the crown and stitch the first layer.

2

Cut more shapes to decorate each square of the band. Appliqué the shapes in layers. Complete the crown design with a second layer of motifs.

3

Machine embroider set stitches in geometric patterns all over both hat pieces.

TO FINISH

Join the short ends of the band to form a tube and stitch to the crown. Make up the lining and place inside the hat, wrong sides facing. Cut the petersham 3 cm (1¼ in) larger than your head measurement plus 1 cm (½ in) seam allowance. Join the short ends and tack (baste) to the lower end of the band. Fold into the hat and top stitch close to the lower edge.

CROWN
25%

HAT BAND
25%

BLACK-AND-WHITE APPLIQUÉ WAISTCOAT

Appliqué a black design on to plain calico to create this striking waistcoat. Draw the design freehand and stitch small sections at a time.

YOU WILL NEED

· · · · · ·

commercial waistcoat pattern

dressmaker's scissors

90 cm x 150 cm
(36 in x 60 in) calico fabric

50 cm x 90 cm
(20 in x 36 in) black cotton

vanishing marker

dressmaker's pins

sewing machine and
black thread

sharp scissors

PREPARATION

Cut out the waistcoat fronts in both calico and black cotton. Cut the waistcoat back in calico only.

1

Draw a design freehand on to the wrong side of the two calico fronts. Use a vanishing marker.

2

Pin the black fronts, right side uppermost, to the right side of the calico fronts. Machine stitch over the drawn lines in black thread.

3

Right side facing and following the design, cut away a small section of the top black layer using sharp scissors. Cut close to the stitching line, to expose the calico below.

TO FINISH

Make up the waistcoat, following the pattern instructions.

4

Carefully machine zig zag over all the raw black edges. Cut and machine until the whole piece has been worked.

PINK-AND-NAVY QUILT

This traditionally styled quilt is made up in hot, modern colours. The backing piece is brought over to the front and joins the sashing and borders to make a self-bound edge.

YOU WILL NEED
. . . . . .

card (cardboard)

craft knife

dressmaker's scissors

50 cm x 90 cm (20 in x 36 in) pink cotton fabric

50 cm x 90 cm (20 in x 36 in) pink-patterned cotton fabric

30 cm x 90 cm (12 in x 36 in) navy-patterned cotton fabric

50 cm x 90 cm (20 in x 36 in) navy cotton fabric

dressmaker's pins

sewing machine and matching thread

iron

1.2 m x 90 cm (48 in x 36 in) wadding (batting)

1.2 m x 90 cm (48 in x 36 in) pink cotton backing fabric

pink and navy quilting thread

crewel needle

PREPARATION

Make card templates 9 cm (3½ in) square. Cut 48 plain pink, 36 pink patterned and 24 navy-patterned fabric squares. Cut four corner templates, 9.5 cm (3¾ in) square, two navy-patterned and two pink. Cut two navy border strips, 9.5 cm x 69 cm (3¾ in x 27¼ in), and two 9.5 cm x 89 cm (3¾ in x 35 in).

1
Arrange the fabric squares and pin together in pairs.

2
Stitch the pairs, using the flag method (see Basic Techniques). Stitch three strips of three squares together to make 12 blocks of nine.

3
Stitch the blocks together, three across and four down. Stitch the corner squares to each end of the short border strips. Press the seams flat. Stitch the long, and then the shorter, borders in place (see Basic Techniques).

4
Trim the wadding (batting) to the same size as the patchwork and sandwich between the patched piece and the backing, right sides out. Pin and tack (baste) through all layers. Bring the backing over to the front, mitre the corners (see Basic Techniques) and slip-stitch to the border. Using the quilting thread, make little navy knots in the centre of each plain pink square and pink knots along the borders.

SIMPLE PATCHWORK CUSHION COVER
· · · · · ·

Squares of fabric, decorated with buttons, are very effective in these hot, sizzling colours. Finish the corners with pompons. Make the cushion in cotton, satin or velvet.

YOU WILL NEED
· · · · · ·

10 cm x 90 cm (4 in x 36 in) pink fabric

10 cm x 90 cm (4 in x 36 in) orange fabric

10 cm x 90 cm (4 in x 36 in) yellow fabric

dressmaker's scissors

30 cm x 90 cm (12 in x 36 in) backing fabric

dressmaker's pins

sewing machine and matching thread

iron

pink, orange and yellow embroidery thread

crewel needle

9 buttons

4 pompons

PREPARATION

Cut out a total of 16 pink, orange and yellow 9.5 cm (3¾ in) squares. Cut the backing fabric in half to measure 30 cm x 45 cm (12 in x 18 in). Turn under a narrow hem on one short side of each piece.

1

Pin the squares in pairs of different colours. Using the flag method (see Basic Techniques), join in strips of four with a 1 cm (½ in) seam. Press the seams open.

2

Pin and stitch the strips together. Press the seams open.

3

Decorate each square with a row of running stitches round the edge in a contrasting colour. Sew a button to each corner, as shown.

4

Right sides facing, pin the backing fabric to the square patchwork, with one piece slightly overlapping the other. Stitch all the seams. Clip the corners, press and turn right side out. Stitch a pompon to each corner.

SATIN DUFFEL BAG

The checker board effect of this patchwork design is enhanced by using strong contrasting colours. The satin is backed with calico, but interfacing could be used instead.

YOU WILL NEED
• • • • • •

50 cm x 90 cm (20 in x 36 in) calico

dressmaker's scissors

1 m x 90 cm (1 yd x 36 in) black satin fabric

50 cm x 90 cm (20 in x 36 in) yellow satin fabric

needle and tacking (basting) thread

sewing machine and matching thread

50 cm x 90 cm (20 in x 36 in) cotton lining fabric

iron

dressmaker's pins

8 eyelets (grommets)

hammer

1.5 m (1¾ yd) silk cord

PREPARATION

Cut out 36 calico 5 cm (2½ in) squares. Tack (baste) half of the squares to the black satin, and half to the yellow satin. Cut 18 yellow and 18 black squares. Using the flag method (see Basic Techniques), stitch into strips of three, alternating black with yellow. Join the strips into one piece, 12 squares by three. Press the seams. Cut a round base 22 cm (8½ in) in diameter and back with calico cut to the same size. Cut out a rectangle the same size as the patchwork and a base in lining fabric.

1

Cut two strips of black satin 7 cm x 38 cm (2¾ in x 15 in). Press under a 1 cm (½ in) turning, pin and top stitch to either end of the patched piece. Stitch the short ends of the patched piece to form a tube.

2

Pin and stitch the base into the tube. Make up a lining in the same way. Right sides facing, pin the lining to the bag along the top edge. Stitch along the top edge of the bag, leaving a small gap. Clip, press and pull through. Close the gap and top stitch 5 mm (¼ in) from the top.

3

Attach seven equally spaced eyelets (grommets) round the top edge. Fold a satin square into three. Fold the ends in and stitch. Top stitch round the bottom of the bag and attach the remaining eyelets. Thread the cord through the eyelets and tie in a knot.

DIAMOND-IN-A-SQUARE SATIN PURSE
· · · · · ·

This opulent evening purse is made from a patched piece of richly coloured satin fabric. Follow the diagram at the back of the book for the arrangement of the patches.

YOU WILL NEED
· · · · · ·

paper and pencil

20 cm x 90 cm (8 in x 36 in) satin fabric, in four colours

dressmaker's scissors

iron-on interfacing

iron

dressmaker's pins

sewing machine and matching thread

20 cm x 30 cm (8 in x 12 in) lining fabric

50 cm (20 in) silk cord

gold bead, with a large hole

PREPARATION

Cut out the patchwork pieces, adding a 5 mm (¼ in) seam allowance. Cut two large 2.5 cm (1 in) squares in colour 1. Enlarge the triangle shape and make a paper template. Cut 16 triangles in both colours 2 and 3. Cut eight 4 cm (1½ in) squares in colour 4. Iron interfacing on to the back of all the patches. Following the diagram for reference, pin and stitch four triangles together then stitch a small square to each end. Make another piece the same. Pin and stitch four more triangles together to make a short strip, and repeat to make a second strip. Stitch either side of one large square. Cut a strip for the casing 32 cm x 7 cm (12½ in x 3 in) in colour 4 and a 11.5 cm (4¼ in) diameter circle for the base in colour 4.

1
Pin and stitch the two narrow patchwork strips either side of the wide one to make a square. Make another patch the same way. Right sides facing, stitch together.

2
Stitch the casing strip to the top edge. Press the seams flat. Fold the piece in half and stitch the side seam. Stitch in the base, trim and clip. Make a lining to fit and insert. Top stitch two rows, 5 mm (¼ in) from the top edge and 5 mm (¼ in) apart, to form a channel. Thread the cord through the channel. Thread on the bead and knot. Fringe the ends of the cord.

HEART NEEDLECASE

· · · · · ·

Appliqué a padded heart on to a silk needlecase and embellish it with metallic thread and tiny bugle beads. The needlecase is constructed like a book, with felt pages stitched inside.

YOU WILL NEED
· · · · · ·

paper and pencil

card (cardboard)

paper scissors

6 cm (2½ in) square turquoise silk fabric

19 cm x 12 cm (7½ in x 4¾ in) purple silk fabric

embroidery scissors

needle and tacking (basting) thread

dressmaker's pins

needle and matching thread

scrap of wadding (batting)

metallic thread

embroidery needle

small gold bugle beads

fabric glue

scraps of felt

28 cm (11 in) fine turquoise ribbon

PREPARATION

Trace the heart motif and make a paper template. Cut out two pieces of card (cardboard) 9 cm x 7 cm (3½ in x 2¾ in).

1

Draw round the template on to the turquoise silk and cut out, adding a 5 mm (¼ in) seam allowance. Clip the seam allowance, turn under and tack (baste).

2

Centre the heart on the righthand side of the purple silk rectangle, and appliqué. From the wrong side, slit the fabric behind the heart and fill with wadding (batting). Close the slit. Embellish the heart with metallic thread and bugle beads and the silk with cross stitches.

3

Glue the two pieces of card on to the reverse of the purple silk. Fold over the silk, mitre the corners and stick down. Lay a piece of felt, cut to size, over the pieces of card and slip-stitch (see Basic Techniques) to the silk.

4

Layer felt rectangles for the book paper inside the case. Stitch them together along the fold line. Thread the ribbon through the book from back to front, and tie in a bow.

SNAKES AND LADDERS
· · · · · ·

This patchwork playmat doubles as a snakes and ladders board. It is constructed like a quilt, so you could make it large enough to cover a child's bed.

PREPARATION

Make a 3 cm (1¼ in) square card (cardboard) template. Cut out 100 squares from the cotton fabric, adding a 5 mm (¼ in) seam allowance. Draw snakes, ladders and counters freehand on to the felt scraps and cut out.

TO FINISH

Cut the backing 3 cm (1¼ in) bigger than the mat all round. Wrong sides facing, pin to the mat. Bring the backing over to the front, mitre the corners and stitch the borders (see Basic Techniques).

1
Stitch the squares together in strips of ten. Stitch all ten strips together to make a square.

2
Number the squares, using black embroidery stitches. Appliqué the snakes and ladders on to the mat.

CHILD'S BLANKET

Small children will love to snuggle up under this cosy blanket. It is appliquéd by hand with colourful circles decorated with buttons.

YOU WILL NEED
• • • • • •

blanket fabric

dressmaker's scissors

tapestry wool

crewel needle

saucer

fabric marker

assorted scraps of coloured woollen or blanket fabric

large buttons

<u>1</u>

Cut the blanket to the size required, turn under a small hem and blanket stitch the edge in different colours (see Basic Techniques).

<u>2</u>

Draw round a saucer on to the scraps of fabric and cut out circles. Hand appliqué to the blanket in running stitch. Sew a button to the centre of each circle.

<u>3</u>

Work large cross stitches in a contrasting colour to fill the background fabric.

SHOE BAG

· · · · · ·

Choose an appropriate shoe to appliqué to this witty drawstring bag. A ballet shoe or gym shoe would also look good.

YOU WILL NEED
· · · · · ·

dressmaker's scissors

*50 cm x 90 cm
(20 in x 36 in) cotton fabric*

*sewing machine and
matching thread*

*65 cm x 7 cm (26 in x
2¾ in) contrasting fabric*

iron

paper and pencil

fabric marker

assorted fabric scraps

iron-on fusible bonding web

dressmaker's pins

scrap of narrow ribbon

*50 cm (20 in) of 2.5 cm
(1 in) wide ribbon*

small button

PREPARATION

Cut the fabric to make a rectangle 45 cm x 70 cm (17¾ in x 27½ in). Fold 6.5 cm (2½ in) to the right side on one long edge, and machine stitch. Right sides facing, fold the rectangle in half and stitch round the base and sides of the bag. Turn right side out. Cut a contrasting strip 66 cm x 7 cm (26 in x 2¾ in) and press under a 5 mm (¼ in) hem on the long sides. Enlarge the template of the shoe motif, and trace on to the fabric scraps. Iron on to the bonding web and cut out.

1
Starting at the seam, pin the contrasting strip to the right side of the bag, 5 cm (2 in) from the top. Top stitch the long edges by hand, leaving the short ends open.

2
Peel the backing off the bonding web and iron the shoe to the bag. Decorate the shoe with hand stitches and a small ribbon bow.

3
Thread the contrasting fabric channel with the wide ribbon. Fold under the raw ends of the ribbon, then join together by stitching the button through both ends.

50%

Patchwork Toy Bag

· · · · · ·

Stitch a piece of rainbow patchwork to make into a large toy bag. The colours run in diagonal lines to look like steps.

You Will Need
· · · · · ·

paper and pencil

card (cardboard)

craft knife

scraps of fabric, in six rainbow colours

iron-on interfacing

iron

sewing machine and matching thread

30 cm (12 in) wooden coat hanger

vanishing marker

red paint, optional

Preparation

Make a 10 cm (4 in) square template in card (cardboard) and cut 72 patches from the interfacing. Iron the interfacing to the fabric scraps and cut out, adding a 5 mm (¼ in) seam allowance. Arrange them in diagonal lines to form rainbow steps. Using the flag method (see Basic Techniques), join half of the squares into two blocks, each six by three. Press the seams flat. Make a large block, six squares by six, for the back of the bag.

To Finish

Stitch the two pieces together with a 1 cm (½ in) seam allowance. Clip the corners, press and turn through. Paint the coat hanger, if wished, and fit into the bag.

1

Right sides facing, stitch the two small blocks together along half their length. Press the seam allowance along the opening. Tack (baste) and then top-stitch to neaten the right side.

2

Right sides facing, pin the two bag pieces together. Lay the coat hanger on the top edge and draw round it. Cut along the curved line.

MOSAIC CUSHION
......

This patchwork technique mimics that of mosaic. Small pieces of fabric are sewn together by hand to create an all-over design.

YOU WILL NEED

paper and pencil

craft knife

dressmaker's pins

50 cm x 90 cm (20 in x 36 in) red cotton fabric

scraps of black, grey and white cotton fabric

dressmaker's scissors

needle and tacking (basting) thread

matching thread

embroidery scissors

sewing machine and matching thread

polyester wadding (batting)

1
Enlarge the design and make paper templates of all the shapes. Decide on a colour scheme and mark each shape.

2
Pin the paper templates to the back of the scraps of fabric and cut out, adding a 5 mm (¼ in) seam allowance.

3
Tack (baste) the fabric shapes to the paper templates.

4
Oversew the patches together, using neat whip stitches (see Basic Techniques). Follow the diagram for reference. Work on a small section at a time.

To Finish

Remove the tacking (basting) threads and paper templates, and press the seams flat. Cut the red cotton backing fabric to fit the patched piece and place together, right sides facing. Machine stitch round the edges, leaving a gap. Trim and clip the corners, turn right side out and fill with wadding (batting). Slip-stitch the gap closed.

KITCHEN APRON
• • • • • •

Make a bright apron with an unusual scalloped border and appliqué kitchen utensils on to it with colourful hand stitches.

YOU WILL NEED
paper and pencil
card (cardboard)
craft knife
fabric scraps
iron-on interfacing
iron
75 cm x 90 cm
(30 in x 36 in) cotton fabric
dressmaker's scissors
75 cm x 90 cm
(30 in x 36 in)
contrasting cotton fabric
vanishing marker
embroidery thread
crewel needle
dressmaker's pins
sewing machine and
matching thread
iron
1 m (1 yd) of 8 cm (3 in)
wide ribbon

PREPARATION

Enlarge the knife, fork and spoon motifs and cut out in card (cardboard). Cut a semi-circle in thin card. Iron the interfacing to the reverse of the fabric scraps. Cut a front in cotton fabric, 60 cm x 50 cm (24 in x 20 in). Cut a backing piece in the contrasting fabric to match.

1
Draw round the templates on to the interfacing. Cut out in different colours.

3
Right sides facing, match the front to the backing and pin. Draw round the semi-circle along the reverse of the lower edge, to mark a scalloped line. Machine stitch round three sides, leaving the top open. Clip the corners and the scalloped edge.

5
Fold under the open edge and press. Press the ribbon in half lengthways. Tack (baste) and top stitch round the top edge.

2
Appliqué the motifs to the apron front with large, colourful hand stitches.

4
Turn the apron right side out. Stitch a line of running stitches along the scalloped edge.

50%

APPLIQUÉ PILLOWSLIP

· · · · · · ·

Appliqué these brightly coloured stars and hearts on to a ready-made pillowslip and decorate with simple stitches. This is an easy way to brighten up faded bedlinen.

YOU WILL NEED
paper and pencil
paper scissors
fabric marker
iron-on fusible bonding web
iron
assorted fabric scraps
dressmaker's scissors
pillowslip
assorted embroidery threads
crewel needle

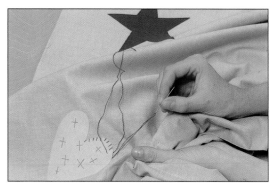

1

Make paper templates of the heart and star motifs. Trace on to the bonding web. Iron the bonding web on to the reverse of the fabric scraps and cut out the motifs.

2

Peel off the backing paper and iron a motif to each corner of the pillowslip. Blanket stitch round the edge (see Basic Techniques) and decorate with embroidery stitches.

3

Sew a running stitch in a contrasting thread on both sides of the pillowcase.

50%

50%

WASH BAG

This little bathroom bag is made from washable fabric. It has a very unusual, asymmetrical patchwork design reminiscent of Art Deco.

YOU WILL NEED

paper and pencil

card (cardboard)

craft knife

dressmaker's scissors

30 cm x 90 cm (12 in x 36 in) white PVC

30 cm x 90 cm (12 in x 36 in) red PVC

30 cm x 90 cm (12 in x 36 in) blue PVC

dressmaker's pins

sewing machine and matching thread

71 cm (28 in) thick white cotton cord

PREPARATION

Enlarge the shapes and cut out in card (cardboard). Following the numbers on the plan, cut out the patches in PVC, adding a 5 mm (¼ in) seam allowance, as follows: cut numbers 1, 6, 13, 14 and 15 in white; 2, 3, 8, 10 and 12 in red; 4, 5, 7, 9 and 11 in blue. Cut a 38 cm x 30 cm (15 in x 12 in) lining in white PVC. Cut a blue PVC 18 cm (7 in) square for the back of the bag.

TO FINISH

Right sides facing, stitch the patch to the blue back piece along one long seam. Stitch the lining to the top of the bag. Clip and trim the seam. Fold in half lengthways and stitch round the seams, leaving a small gap. Pull through then fold in the lining, leaving a 6 cm (2½ in) band at the top. Stitch two parallel lines 5 mm (¼ in) from the top edge, 1 cm (½ in) apart, for the channel. Thread the cord through the channel and knot the ends.

1

The patch is made in two halves. To stitch the first half, join blue 4 to red 2. Join blue 5 to red 3. Next, join 4/2 to white 6. Join 3/5 to white 6. Join the whole piece to white 1.

2

To stitch the second half, join blue 9 to red 10. Join 9/10 to white 14. Join red 10 to blue 11. Join 10/11 to white 13. Join blue 11 to red 12. Join blue 9 to red 8. Join 8/9 to white 15. Join blue 7 to red 8. Stitch the patches together.

50%

HOT WATER BOTTLE COVER

· · · · · ·

Strip patchwork is used for this jazzy cover, which is then quilted with a scroll and diamond pattern.
The layers of padding will help to keep your hot water bottle warm on cold winter nights.

YOU WILL NEED

*1 m x 90 cm
(1 yd x 36 in) white fabric*

dressmaker's scissors

*50 cm x 90 cm
(20 in x 36 in) black fabric*

*sewing machine and
matching thread*

hot water bottle

vanishing marker

*50 cm x 90 cm
(20 in x 36 in)
wadding (batting)*

red thread

*2 m (2 yd) of 2.5 cm (1 in)
black bias binding*

dressmaker's pins

iron

3 press studs (snap fasteners)

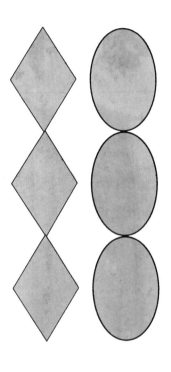

QUILTING DESIGNS 50%

PREPARATION

Cut the white fabric into four and the black into six 50 cm x 7.5 cm (19¾ in x 3 in) strips. Join the strips together lengthways in two sets of five, alternating the colours. Trace round a hot water bottle on to the patched pieces, add a 1 cm (½ in) seam allowance and cut out. Cut out two pieces the same from the white fabric for the lining. Trace and draw the quilting design on to the cover pieces.

1

Sandwich the wadding (batting) between the patched pieces and the lining, right sides facing out. Tack (baste) through all the layers. Stitch round the edge on both pieces. Stitch the quilting design in red.

2

Bind the top edge with the bias binding. Pin another strip of bias binding round the side edges on the right side and stitch to the cover. Bind the second side. Place the two sides together, right sides facing, with the binding sandwiched between. Stitch round the seam line, leaving a 15 cm (6 in) opening at the top. Trim and press.

3

Turn right side out and slip-stitch the opening. Attach the press studs (snap fasteners) to the top edge of the cover.

HEART BROOCH
· · · · · ·

This tiny appliqué heart made from scraps of fabric is embellished with gold thread. Mounted on a brooch back it makes a pretty badge, but it could also be appliquéd directly on to a pocket or the corner of a shirt collar.

YOU WILL NEED

paper and pencil

scrap of gold velvet or silk

sharp embroidery scissors

scraps of blue and grey woollen fabric

iron-on interfacing

iron

sewing machine and gold thread

scrap of cream organza

dressmaker's pins

brooch back

PREPARATION

Draw the heart shape, transfer it to the gold velvet or silk scrap and cut out. Cut a scrap of blue fabric 3 cm x 4 cm (1¼ in x 1½ in), and a scrap of grey fabric, 5 cm x 4 cm (2 in x 1½ in). Iron the grey fabric to the interfacing. Machine several lines of the gold thread in a square to make a frame.

1

Place the blue fabric on to the frame, then the heart, and finally cover with a scrap of organza and pin. Machine stitch the organza to the backing close to the gold frame. Trim the organza back to the stitch line.

2

Pull the interfacing away from round the brooch. Sew the brooch back to the underside.

CHILD'S APRON

This painting apron is constructed from strips of fabric. It has a roomy pocket for pens and paintbrushes, trimmed with pompon tape. This apron is made in cotton, but you could also use stain-resistant PVC fabric.

PREPARATION

Cut five 6 cm x 20 cm (2½ in x 8 in) strips of assorted fabric for the pocket. Draw the apron shape on paper, and cut out in cotton fabric. Machine stitch under a hem all round the apron.

ENLARGE TO THE CHILD'S SIZE

1

Stitch the strips together to make one piece. Cut a piece of cotton fabric to the same size. Right sides facing, pin and stitch the seams, leaving a small gap. Clip the corners, press and turn through.

2

Slip-stitch the pompon tape to the top edge of the patched piece.

3

Tack (baste) the pocket to the apron and top stitch.

4

Press the ribbon in half lengthways. Cut a 61 cm (24 in) length and sew to either side of the top edge. Cut the rest of ribbon in half and sew either side of the waist. Neaten the ends.

PVC Bag

This bag shows how unusual fabrics can create an effect completely different to traditional patchwork. Clip the curved seams to ensure a smooth fit.

You Will Need

paper and pencil

card (cardboard)

craft knife

dressmaker's scissors

1 m (1 yd) wadding (batting)

*1 m x 90 cm
(1 yd x 36 in) blue PVC*

*50 cm x 90 cm
(20 in x 36 in) red PVC*

*50 cm x 90 cm
(20 in x 36 in) white PVC*

dressmaker's pins

*sewing machine and
matching thread*

iron

*needle and tacking
(basting) thread*

knitting needle

To Finish

Stitch the side edges of the patched pieces to make a tube. Pin and stitch in the base. Trim and clip the seams. Pin the handles to the bag. Stitch the blue PVC lining to the top of the bag, securing the handles at the same time and leaving a 7.5 cm (3 in) gap. Pull the lining through and slip-stitch the gap. Press the bag under paper.

PREPARATION

Enlarge the design from the back of the book and cut out two complete bag pieces in blue PVC for the lining and a wadding (batting) piece, adding a 1 cm (½ in) seam allowance. Cut out two of each patch shape in red and white PVC, adding 5 mm (¼ in) seam allowance. Cut a red and blue PVC base and a wadding base, adding a 1 cm (½ in) seam allowance. Cut two red handles 36 cm x 10 cm (14 in x 4 in).

1

Join patches, 1 and 3 to 2. Join 4 and 6 to 5. Join 7 and 9 to 8, and 10 and 12 to 11. Clip, and press the seams carefully under a piece of paper, using a cool iron. Join together to make two large squares, then join the squares together. Make two pieces the same. Clip and press the seams flat.

2

Place the two patched pieces and the red base on to the wadding (batting), and tack (baste) round the edges.

3

Make up the blue PVC lining.

4

Stitch the red handle strips lengthways. Turn through and fill with wadding (batting), using a knitting needle. Pull through the wadding and trim off 2½ cm (1 in) at the ends.

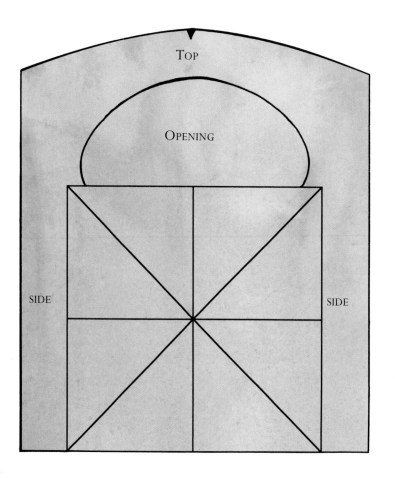

TOP

OPENING

SIDE

SIDE

1950S BISTRO TABLE
MATS P. 32

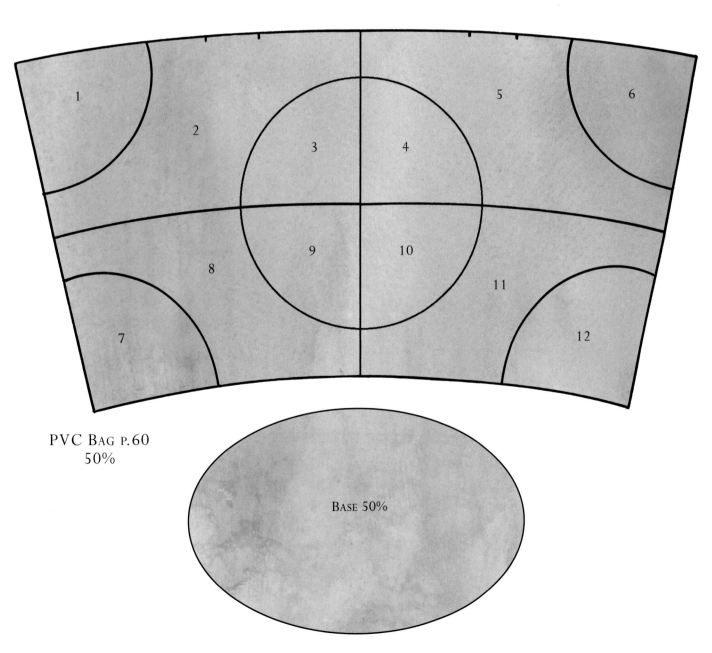

DIAMOND-IN-A-
SQUARE SATIN
PURSE P.43 50%

PVC BAG P.60
50%

BASE 50%

INDEX
......

ACKNOWLEDGEMENTS
......

The Publishers would like to thank the following craftspeople who designed and made the projects for this book: Petra Boase, Julia Crook, Joanna Davies, Rachel Frost, Lucinda Ganderton, Judith Izatt, Sylvia Landers, Teresa Searle and Isabel Stanley. Additional photography by Debbie Patterson, pages 6 t and 7; and Peter Williams, page 6 b.